THE CROWS OF AFTER

EXSANGUINE HART

Names, places, events and characters are used fictitiously. Any resemblance to anything (or anyone), living or dead is entirely coincidental.

Copyright © May 2022, Exsanguine Hart

All rights reserved. No part of this book may be stored, transmitted or reproduced without written permission from the author or publisher, excepting the use of quotations in a book review.

First edition paperback May 2022

ISBN paperback: 978-1-7779303-0-1
ISBN ebook: 978-1-7779303-1-8

Book design, cover design by Exsanguine Hart.

Published by Specimen SandWitch Press
specimensandwitch.com

Contents

Start of the Circle 1
In the Ragged Tracks You Tread 2
Smell of Pies 4
Indecision 6
Waiting Game 8
Floor Plans 10
Ode to a Moth 12
The Race 17
Count 18
Skin 20
Anything Can 21
The Great Oxymoron of Life 24
Curiosity 25
Oracle 26
H(a)unted 28
Dysfunction 29
At a Convenience Store in the Outside World 30
Back Door 32
Sleep 33
Wander 34
Lost and Found at the Edge of a Trail 36
Fable 37
Let's Travel to the Desert 40
Autopsy 42

Ghoul, And,	43
Accumulated	45
Music Box	46
A Picnic	48
Falling Apart	49
Symbiose	50
Trail of Laughs	52
Source	55
Whisper of Fancy	56
Bread	57
Awake	58
Ditty	60
Tout un Monde dans ma Main Gantée	62
The Art of Contagion	64
Rain Viewing	65
Digest	66
Maggots Rise	68
Haunt	70
After	72
Scavengers	74

A Collection of Horrors

Start of the Circle

The four fell through the floor, into
a field of terrified scarecrows.
Fragmented, the strawpeople had earned
an entourage of jovial crows,
messengers to mark them out of place.

Dips in the field created
an uncanny valley of
pitchforked emotions, alarms that
brought wolves from the trees.

Strewn up, as they are
conscious but not real—
who is to suffer; we
or the crows we've deprived of a meal?

In the Ragged Tracks You Tread

i am told to follow
a mold of achievements
at the dinner table, seated between two

frozen automatons, rusted joints extending to utopia;
i listen to the tales they would tell were they
alive like me.
Dirt drips from their fingertips.
One would think
my companions knew success as it filled their stomachs
and laid them to rest. The print on their torsos
matches the star charts and trophies set out
in place of cups.
Too heavy to drink from, i
swallow
my thirst.

Meanwhile,
the mold says to be
grateful for the wheat scythed down to fill the plates.
Depictions of the automatons litter this house on the
field, depictions
of reapers on the plains while inside
five sets of wilted plants prove

devotion to hard work.
True work, and the models tell me where to find
true evil;

evil—the world
evil—the people

here there is no evil only
perfect dust to arrange into flowers with sand-rakes, a
stillness in calm locust trills and perfect sink filled with
dishes to be washed by hot water when i wander into
the kitchen. Hot water and
soap. Empty my mouth so that i speak cleanly.
Scald my skin
in rank with the kneeling dolls

Smell of Pies

Fifteen crows baked into a pie.
A smell seeps through the undergrowth, through
endless wheat stalks to sunrise, lured towards
the house that breaks horizons.
Smell of pies.
Smell of home.
Put to bed by a mannequin, ignore
the shadows that flit from the crust
and play pretend.

i hang up a face on the bedpost, eyes closed to a bed-
time story murmured by sand-winds.
      "Ignore the crows/they're only out to mangle
the truth and the children/pretend
      they won't come to visit."

In my dreams the dolls buy tickets to the oven-show
and stand there, statue-like, beatless, while the crowd
combusts and meets the birds like so many gaseous
wraiths.

We play in the back shed with its drought-caressed
shingles and dead signs, an unstable structure.
i play with the dolls, restraints in their stares as i let
them place
their cold hands on my arm.

THE CROWS OF AFTER

The heat is off
but the caress of wood
and porcelain offers warmth.

We learn to be as real as
the smell of pies,
pretending a skill to be worn
by sweaty handprints, clawed crow-marks
embedded in tempered glass,
the oven door, all
that is needed to claim a life

Indecision

The gate is really a contraption slipping between cage
and barbed wire, a bird-trap confusing
a beacon of screams with calls for attention

Like
s
    e
        n
            t
        r
   i
e
   s
    they hang from the hooks in the shed with their catch,
                          the crawlspace creatures,
                                tomorrow's dinner.
                    Exhaustion and damp cloths
                  peel the sweat from their skin

                                i mimic them, invisible.
                      Impale myself on the bars trying
                                  to be noticed

run, the rats grow
fangs and sing the
venom of
their victo-
ry/don't
run/just-
Crawl, or
you'll
fall
to-
o
;

Waiting Game

Wait
with one eye open
one eye closed,
+senses.

(A mechanical nurse paints
me blue.)

Wait
with one eye closed,
and one glued shut;
i feel
the pressures
swim around me.

(Her metal arm pulls up the splint. It chafes my
scratches, my fluids pooling in the weave. Pus,
crocheted with my blood. i imagine she tells me to be
better, for /next time/
Infection will cure me.)

Wait.
Anticipation is
a game+five experience
delete experience./

THE CROWS OF AFTER

To feel (un)
needed.

(If i fail, there are others who are better. She collapses
the room and the room tells me the world is made of
paper.)

Wait,
and be warned
+eyes shut tight before their knives.
They marvel at my repugnance.

Criss-crossed with my stripped off lies

(reschedule my penance,
but don't be caught.)

Floor Plans

Good hiding places
are dark and warm,
with little room to breathe.
                        A monarch among dead moths
                           places a crown on the floor
                            to see which mouse gets to it first
                                wishing to be that small.
The mice wonder
why the doors all lock from outside
are mummified in the heat
waiting to be let out.
                            The hiding place creaks
                                it lives in each wall
                                concrete and hollow.

A moth walks out on Death
it was a bad double date
and no one liked each other
except Persephone
Persephone liked herself.
                        The crows covet snowflakes,
                            their spiderweb cutouts.
                             The crows take the crown
                                  for the greater good

BECOMING THE VOID

Ode to a Moth

Dark moth, are you the cure,
or painting of my loneliness?
You have no shelter, washed in
a dredge of curses. You own only
the hell-thorned monster
that precedes your reputation,
evil-eyes that sleep upon your back.
You plot meticulously to conquer
every day in abject misery.

You hide your face in fungus leeching
off the fire-bark. (Claim wonders
for your skin concealed in trees.) Directional
selection haunts your snappish senses,
such that silver-shining leaves adorn
each bough refusing to reflect
your melancholy

You do nothing, fear unlikely
thoughts of your existence,
spreading through the moss
into the tiger-grass where you have made your bed
and plan to lie, awake or dead irrelevant in desperate
shadows of the flies, so ignorant
of your study on their happiness.

THE CROWS OF AFTER

Your jealousy leads nowhere. Stay
here, tremble in the moonlight. It
illuminates your path to anonymity,
this form that will erase each aspect
of your sorrows.

You butterfly of the night,
you think it better, as do i,
you'd rather never had become.
You fear the pain around and wish for none

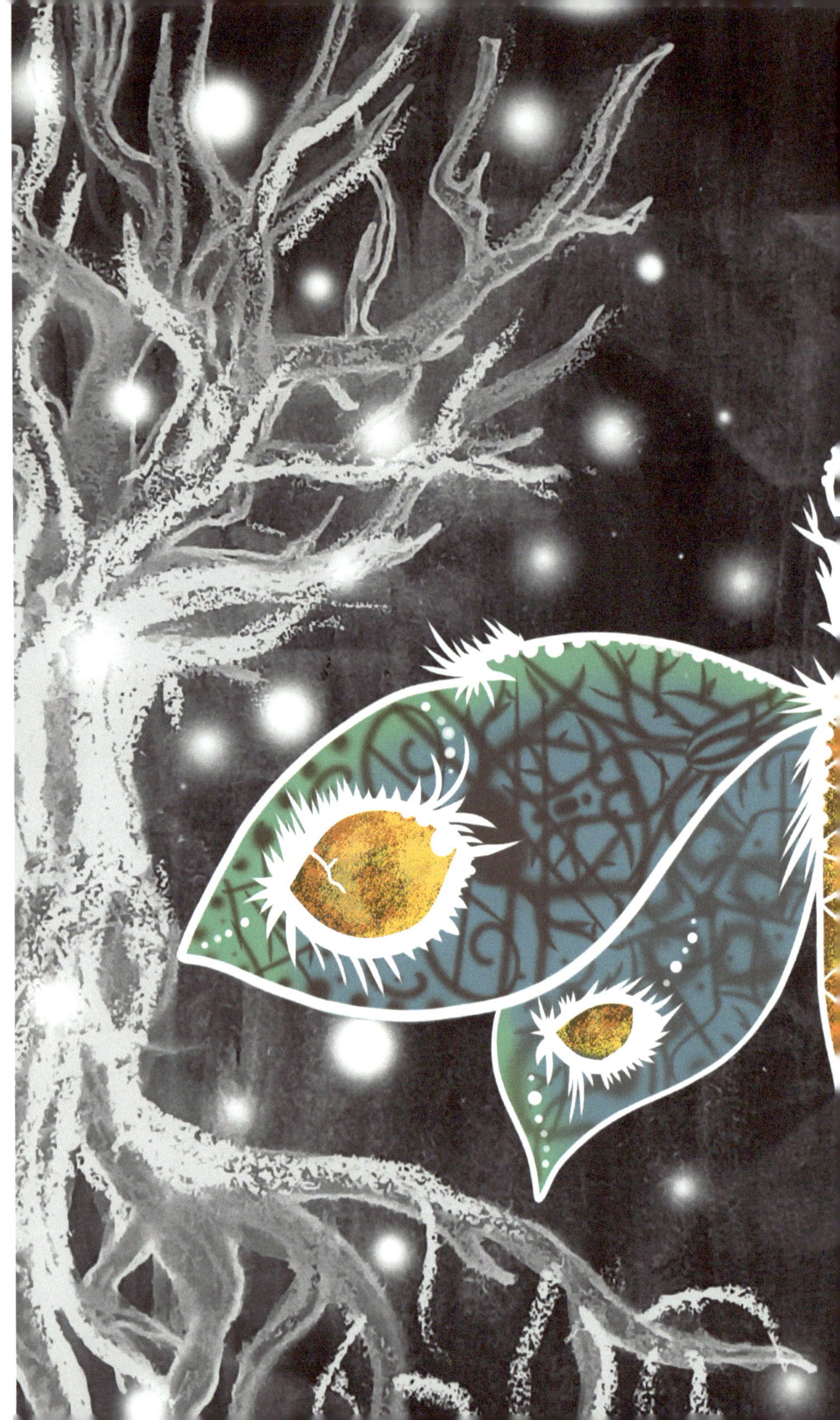

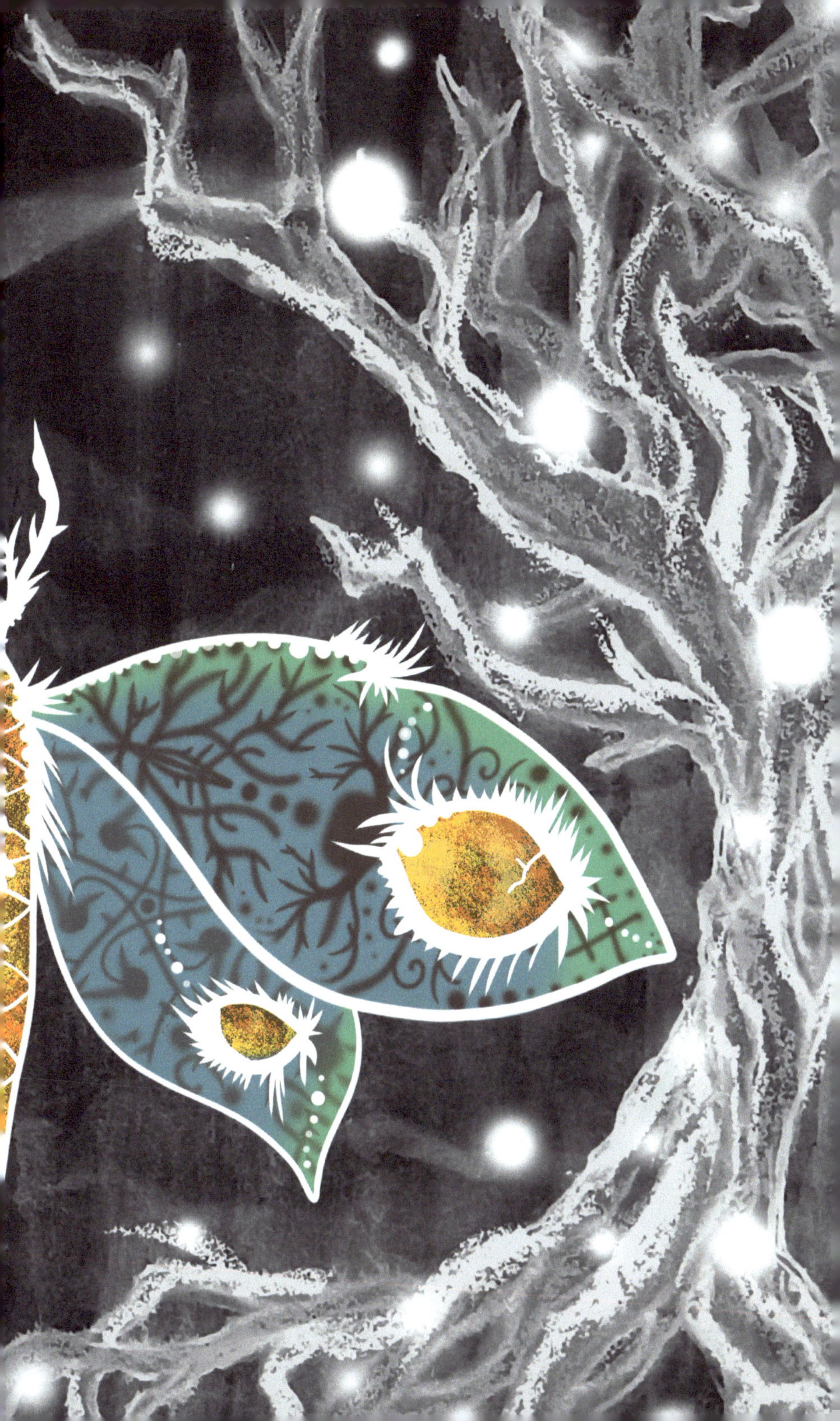

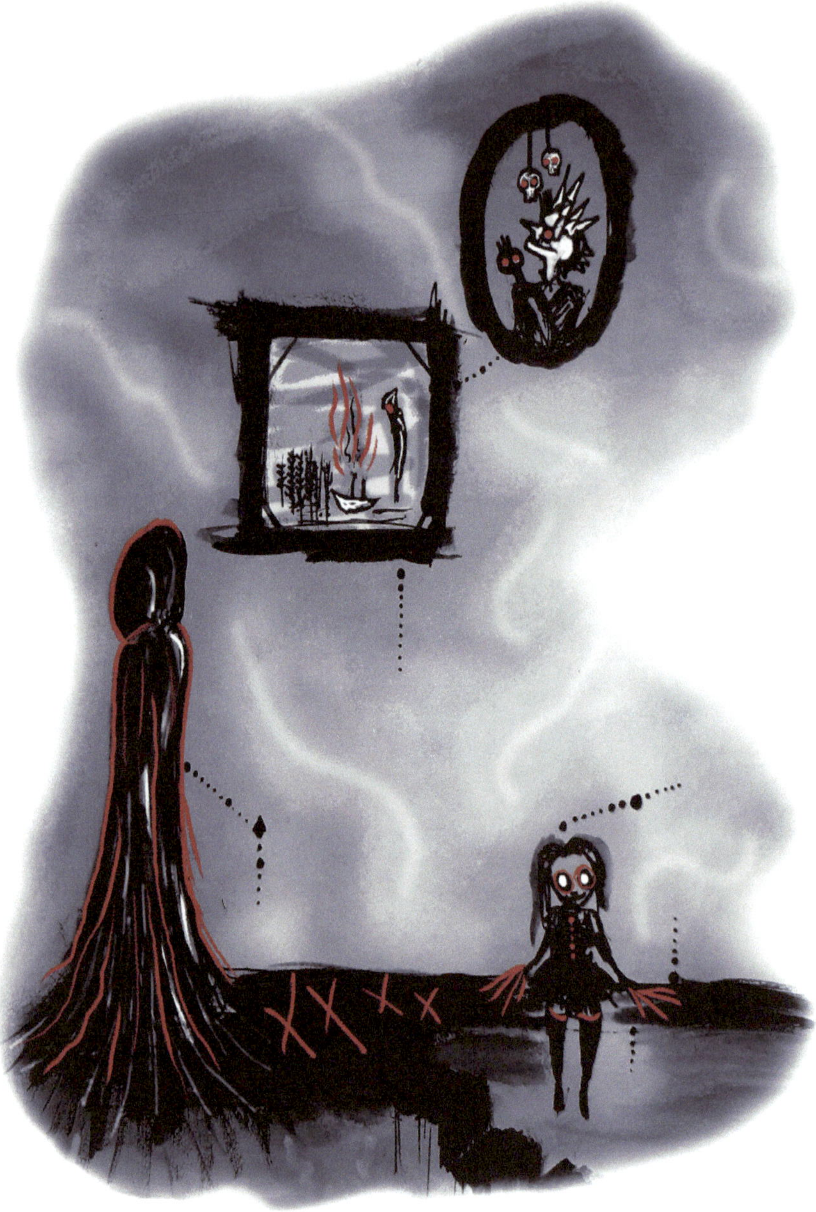

The Race

Whatever disgrace
i am guilty of holds

the attention of the sandpapered doll at the doorway.
When i turn away, stilted motion between smooth
joints (the rustle of vermin, whispers
in the crawlspace) will capture failure and deliver it
to the mechanical nurse, a new evil, a new
part to replace until i no longer break the machine.

This time my head.
This time my head.

Grating against my faults a presence causes
the sandpapered doll to fall down the stairs,
away from here, away from the failure, away

from the mess room.
Filled with the equals,
merchants and criminals
barter my doubt and
contort it.

Assassins are needed
to kill it—before it kills me

Count

*I first met Remorse at the window, six
more holes in her face than there should have been, grey skin
protected by rags.
Since then i've seen
Remorse
at every high place:
The bridge. The slow-moving escalator.*

Regretting the jump.

She digs into me with her iron nails. In
the name of improvement i
allow her to claw out the thoughts that i hate
(suspended)
i hate her not i
hate
(last inch to let go)
my thoughts

i gift her my maggots and watch her
tear them into gruesome figures.
She gives them mouths and puts them to my ear
to exorcise shortcomings, a new Malleus.
Maleficarum! i'll fall if she stumbles.
In hindsight
i'm begging Remorse to
rewind.

Skin

Shapeshifter
shift yourself
into the higher
monster,
higher stakes.

We live in awe.
On veut apprendre.
First and only circus.

The diners learn to match the moths.
Their lightweight limbs make sounds
like hollow drums against the floor. They spread
their dirty wings across the walls, in sync with me.
We turn in circles; murmured rituals make the flying
last/a late abomination we have stolen
(over supper) from its honest blueprint,
chiseled into our
deceitful bones

Anything Can

Cold is
a trail to Pain,
chained in a clearing choked by trees.
Otherwise alone, she keeps a party of Shadows/
Shapeshifters, stirring company with fire
and misused mannequins, collections
of failed metamorphoses.

(The crows loom closer, positions of sight in the tree-roots commingled with darkness.)
The Shadows dress
as the nurse did, search for
the subject of unplanned extraction
with their drills and dull daggers
and stones.

i dress myself in shame
for the operation.

Rocks were made to
rearrange/recycle/repurpose/reuse sun-bleached
bones into weapons.
Pain derives error. Draws blood
on the edge of disguise. Paints over my eyes,
again.

(Look to the forest in flames,
at the edge of the field,
imaginary beings leading
in dealings of reconstruction)

MIXED MESSAGES

MIXED

The Great Oxymoron of Life

They taught me to look up,
    (great seers, wizards in the world of science)
up at what i could become
    (handing out apples embellished with
Newton's laws)
up into the tree of
nevermind
    (their faces sallow and bored of their silence)
and accomplishments—
    (their hands full, but Atlas could carry the
world, so why shouldn't they?)
Another diploma to fly like an uncapped balloon
    (their hats thrown in the air, into the distance,
their wooden youth)
but no one ever told me to look down
    (ever told me anything)
    their faces cryptid, disapproving
but isn't under the ground
    (they carry the crypt keys between their teeth)
where we'll all end
Up?

Curiosity

i timidly open the drawer
to touch what has never been named
the one-eyed fish from the deep Mariana
the tiger that in life was tamed

the mermen that swam in the river,
(made of torn-apart dolphin fins)
and the glass eye that surely,
it can't be denied…
(The ending to this one was grim.)

Disassemble invisible puzzles
i marvel at ships in the air—
the certificate of the collector
is the proof stamped on everything here.

Gilded skulls of doctored monstrosities—
but the buttermoths under the glass
would suggest that there are no veracities
in this cabinet of curiosities

Oracle

Droning/dripping in reverb. Howls rising in/to the
Evers. Fresh/flesh offerings. Things
are not what they seem. Things/
are/not what they
seem.
Quiet chorus in reverence
cathedral in flames for the oracle. Cathedral/ in
flames. Burning. Rising. Light. See?
Can't you/See?
i wish
the pictures on the wall would
speak to me,
oh Oracle-let/
me See
too

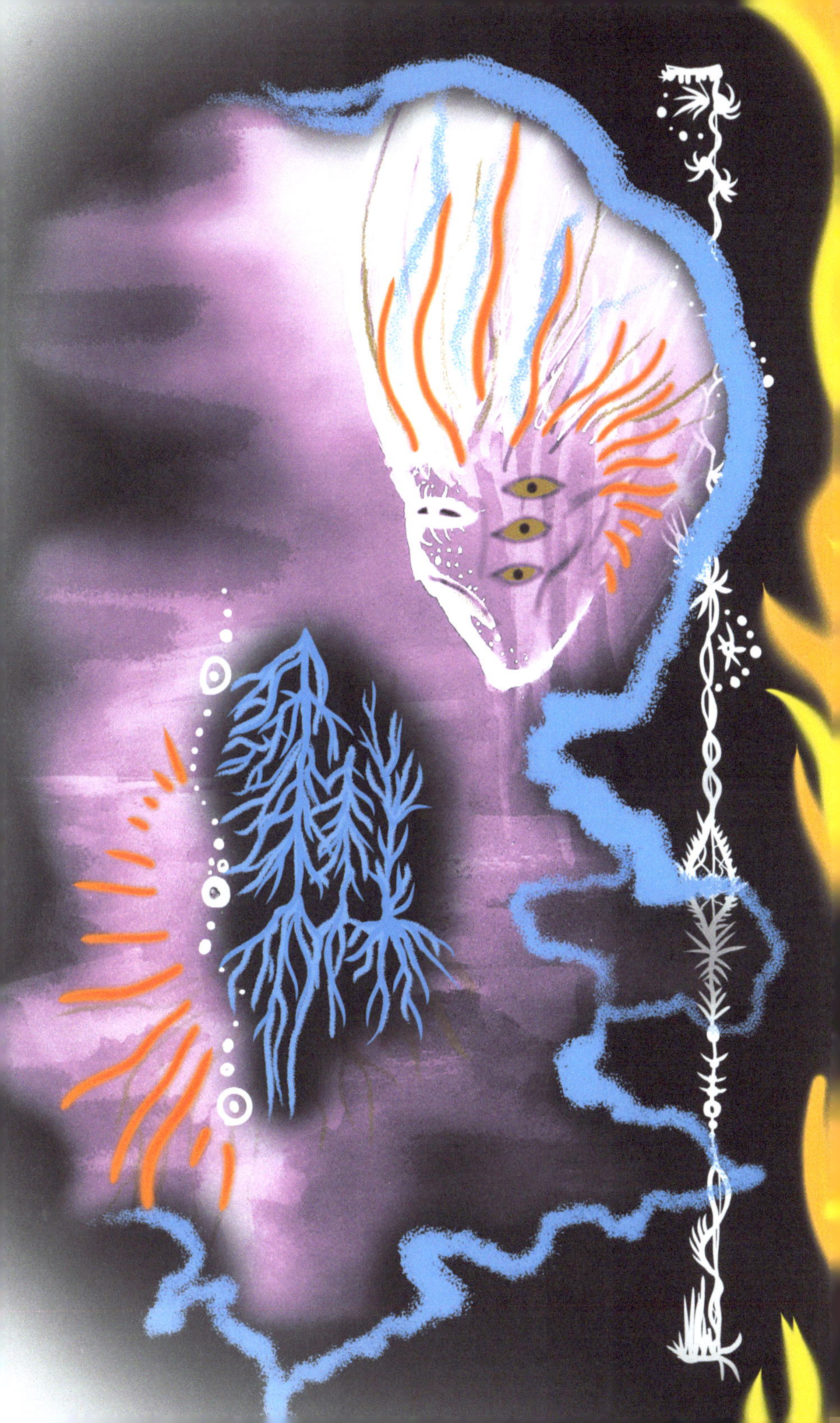

H(a)unted

Shutters are made to open,
and block off the moment another looks in.
They are photograph shy and
so easy to stick with a needle/unsanitized pin.
There should be a roundabout way to
tear open the skin
but look in through the ghost,
high grained blur, every mark on the printout a sin

Dysfunction

Sounds
pile up,
threatening silence.
i argued with
the automatons
over

a swallowed occurrence,
regularities.

Where no word drains life out of a place...
Carbon monoxide
breath, sweeter than the death
of decent conversation.
Trapped between four walls and an open door and
a window cut out for a five-cent show, Blame,
shatter not the house
but the dreams inside it

At a Convenience Store in the Outside World

Tip lump of melting butter fresh off the shelf.
    The cashier is at the front.
i patter over sceptic reincarnation,
into the smashed skull, equal fated candy bars.
i grin panic into disillusionment,
rough cries into the skeletal burns
that hang from stretched hairs of simplicity side
by side with
the deflated balloon.

"Here's the change—

a penny for your thoughts?"

DREAM SEGMENTS

Back Door

i answered at the door to knocking,
knocking from inside my head.
Suburban sidewalk cracks
will tell me nothing/suffering
passed in the dusk/has passed the red door
dread! i heard a knocking—
file into safety in the admass.
(Confide!) i hunch-backed shut the blinds on
creeping eyes, my
neighbor demon screeching/more in store
they wait outside/their
knuckles crack on knocking
fading in and out of vision/thunderclaps
smelt summer rain
i swear i heard a knocking there,
an endless knocking that accompanies my
brain/i let them in
my door is red

Sleep

Comfort in the soft
caress of brick
it pillows my cheek
my wrist snaps into
buzzing
piping blights the sands

sliced
home wood
no-one sits behind the wall
close dances over lipids
quiver under seas
the swinging birds
lay dust uncial

i dial
sameness
stinging pools
of dim
soliloquies

is all drowned out into
euphonic liberty/i stare
into the
void

Wander

Running down the wall head first,
would it not be much better not to be?
Turn round, stare
at the nothing past me.
The lamp post went off
for a time.

No one tells us to wander
the tracks we cross out of necessity.

Everything is shredded by the train
too late/arrived at last,
screeching over splintered
level crossings.

i'll be catcalled on the fourth.
It breaks the snow.
It breaks perfected solitude
immersed in ordinary things.

(The clouds at night, the manhole caps)

THE CROWS OF AFTER

Perhaps there's something in the sewers
getting to the bottom of a jar
of thrown out conversations, marbles
smiling on the air.

Racoons live in the dumps of human consciousness.
Their eyes reflect the bark, the cyclist,
stop sign
in slow motion.

(The roadkill it won't touch
for it twitches and grins.)

The tree has been there for a day.
Has nothing changed?
i pass the midnight walk over the
aging cobblestones,
into the witching hour of thought.

In absent light, where has my shadow gone?

one. The slime depletes the energy in stores of liberation. It flowers i
moldand bookshelves lined with grave goods and half scarring, putrid
dies, spreads walking rot into rebirthed impermanence to find the one at

Lost and Found at the Edge of a Trail

thers at/ feathers at/ feathers at/ feathers at/ feathers at/ feathers at/ feathers

FAULT

ers/of the feathers/of h thers/of the feathers/of the
the feathers of the feathers of the feathers of the feath
the feathers/of the feath rs/of the feathers/of the fea
ers of the feathers of the feat of the feathers of the feathe

athers at/ feathers at/ feathers at/ feathers at/ feathers at/ feathers at/ feath

Cursed odour crawls in line, claws out from bruising organs, thousand
that rip at mottled afters. They drip formaldehyde reincarnate into ca
orous desire. Breaking fever boils waves of the undead; or was that a

Fable

The crows watched
four children, one wearing a cat scratch honour mark
buying a half-pound bag of friandises. They
proceeded to drop out the liquorice pieces
"Foul flavour" they said,
un par un par un par un par
un/a new tarmac for boots weighed in tenseness.
Watched it come alive, and sickly December light rays
passed through their eyes as the diablerie melted
around them in circles.
Invisible edges prodding
at revelations they started to spin
towards. Just Towards, around&around&around&around&around
spilled inside or outside in?
(Cercueil ouvert)
coating the walls, their hands
dulling off into sea salt greys and skipping back
into black through ten dimensions, it coated the cat
they had strangled[1] earlier
that afternoon, (droop-whiskered cadavre)/tailtied
against the blue rafters, they watched
It come alive,
coated in death...

---

1 *murdered*

Exsanguine Hart

It unfolded itself, rearranged its bones into
what could be described as a cat again, rough matted fur,
un visage craintif
shared between them all. It stalked through them, Janus,
a two-faced demon marked off by tail flicks, a hissing
speech. They forgot
their scrapes and the corner store, the industrial barn they
had sent to the flames.
Nine was the only thing they'd ever known.
It frayed away the frequency, a conscious, dying wave of
visions./
Nine lives. Nine lives. Neuf chats seemed to pass in
an endless stream of deja vu and they
knew without thinking to jump
into the burning pool, to be
one with the chat,
one with death,
un with Nine.
IX
9

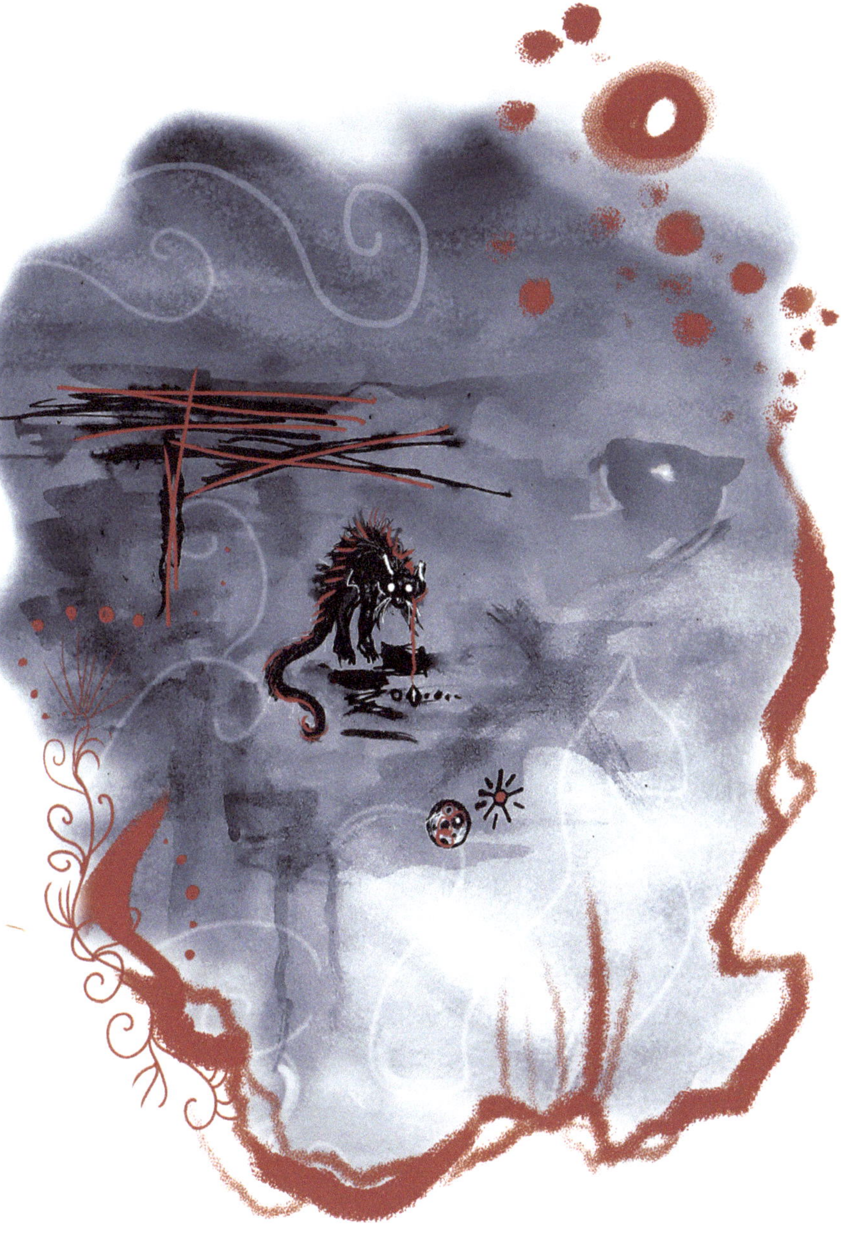

Let's Travel to the Desert

Call to me/patter of footsteps/pattern of innocence; i am/held fast in this collection of oddities. What will become of me what! What? Shout it/again and again and again, i. Fear they did not hear/lost ears/lost fears. Lost and buried in the snowdrifts. i went to a river, a mother of fish, gleaming. She has run away and i am left between two riverbanks, tearing my hands against the frozen mud. Time makes me a desert and i marvel at myself, a still life landscape. i am rebuilt where the world turns blue, turns into cerulean paper, where water forgets to answer the tide/my river forgets to rush over my sand dunes and i forget too. Cut the tether here/forevers calling (hear them call to me). Silent foot steps shudder aching bones in lasting tremors (oh the earth is spinning), spinning wisely. Reassurance. Nights melt on my cheek as reminiscent footsteps ring, bells falling/stalling in the snow. In snow. In cold. In trees.

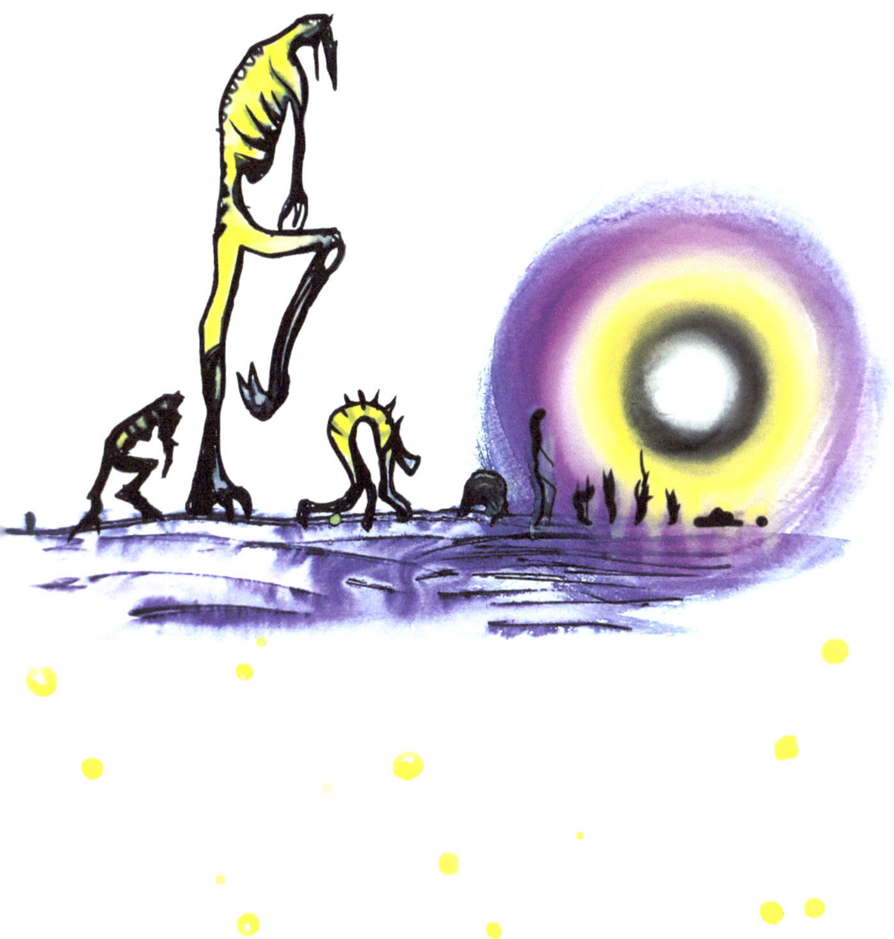

Autopsy

Y-cut,
T-shaped incision as i was taught,
the mechanical nurse guiding my hand
with the blade as i drive the scalpel again i
disfigure rotten flesh.
The practice corpses, she'd tell me,
were mauled by crows.

Snip.
Pump air into the stillborn lungs—

the straw man was disemboweled,
she'd say, a montage of unprepared entrails

but only her metal arm speaks as it creaks, pointing
to the garbage pail stood beneath the window,
waiting to forget the smell.

Ghoul, And,

There is a ghoul without a face
without a name, without a place
who waits as all the rest pass by
those who with eager hand await,
with eager eye
the prey led through pearlescent gates,
the drunken bait heaved through the door.
(Be ripped apart, uneven as its gait.)
Four crows that feed
have not a chance to see past grimace and despair
that sinks the prey into its reverie.

The faceless ghoul thinks on
does nothing still
beyond all sense of self,
all selfless will

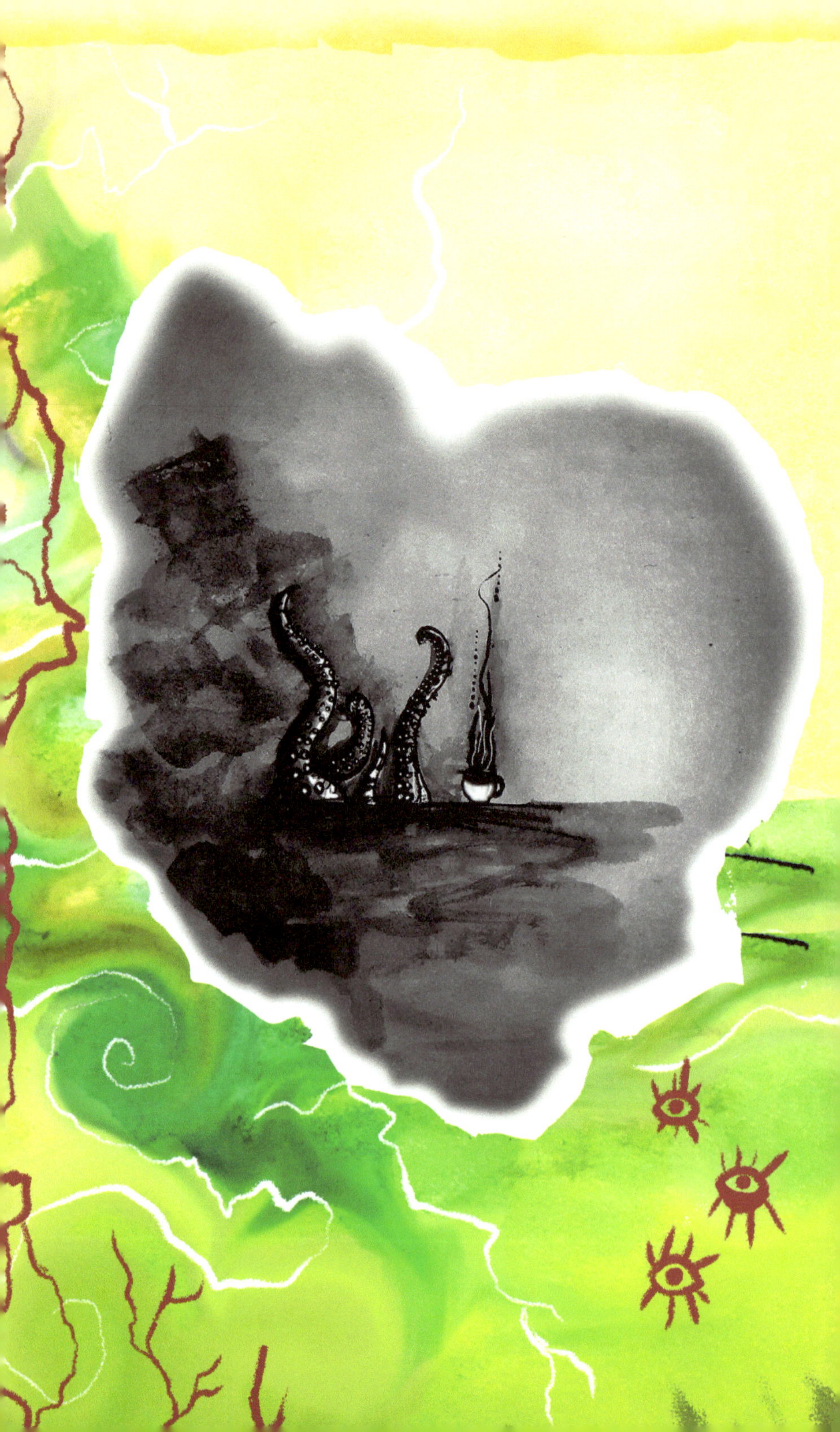

Accumulated

Red eyes at night don't scare,
in familiar light, but i know that
nothing has eyes here, nothing that sees,
not anymore,
in any case.

They tuck letters
of disappointment into
the corners of their lips, their
hidden sleeves,
to shut away for later.

And the tentacles pushing their way through the floor
are just the new rug,
(are pulling the wind through the door)
                    the door that is dripping with blood!

                    The visitor nods,
         sees only a brand-new blue rug.

Music Box

It's cramped inside this box,
repeating cranks upon the pewter handle
bringing worn down sound
into the clocks.
Each tinkle of the bell procures
a wooden fever.
Shining coins conjure disheartened jacks;
i turn the wheel. They are the sickly here as

i help in the packing room:
i put their pieces together, to leave to the crows.
i help
i turn the wheel, the sentience grinder.
i turn the rack,
or these fiends would move on their own, they would
come alive and cut through the wheat in the spring,
they would
fracture the song.

Then, they were falling.
Falling apart, falling
into the groans of a greater machine,
disparus dans le noir

Round and Round and Round and Round we go...
NUQNEH NUQNEH NUKNEH NUKNEH NUQNEH...

Is there an Elsewhere?

[there are rats about]

IS THERE AN EARTH AND A WONDERFUL WORLD

THE IMMORTAL

IS THERE AN ELSEWHERE

HOW MUCH MASS TO MAKE ELSEWHERE / MAKE PLAN
ELSEWHERE
[and what a wonderful world is out there]

ELSEWHERE

low in rats
EVERY LITTLE THING SHE SAID [SHE SAID]

our rats are very low
very rats low
rats very
veery
veering

NEVER HAVE I EVER...

WRONG

A Picnic

Little interlude;

A tea party on yellow grass, burnt umber, sepia.
"Picture perfect," a drawn-on
Victorian painting.

A circuit condemning the flames and
conducting revulsion.
They said it was real, late guests, brass cogs
and the missing breeze and the blanket
that welcomed processions of nettles.

Each dish is perfect for the ants in coattailed suits
to eat a spread of sand arranged in glasswork,
iron face-shapes
(reignite the sun for it)
brought along for me, i hope/
i hope not no one.

Falling Apart

The dolls don't feel safe anymore.

They huddle together, wiping cobwebs
from the cracked window frames to stare
at the outside, its unyielding winds.

(Before the leaves begin to fall.
Before old flowers wilt and die.)

A storm approaching, four crows
are at the bayonet. Soon it will snow
their ashes. Soon there will be no door.

(Before the fields are blown away
before old battlements turn to beetles
before glass wings and crushed shells
are scattered into obscurity.)

They don't feel safe anymore.

Symbiose

Wind waffles in the window box
where Thicket and Thatch, deserted dolls
listen to the flowers sing.

Morning Glories, Poison Oak,
Gardenia and Lilac,

castle terrace where a Crow swings,
sipping coffee through its bandaged,
broken beak. And candied

Clematis and Roses,
Allium, Sage, pollinate

ruffles and lace and bisque faces,
straw hats, silver locks and slips. The garden
winds Thatch and Thicket, the fairies

and listens to them sing.

THICKET & THATCH

Trail of Laughs

Resurrected to the table
glances and reawakenings make
it hard to remember which wood
is the right wood to build scarecrows.

Tie off their heads and choke them to their posts.
A frenzy for the crows/sharp beaks/harsh breaths
surprise-etched vignettes on the mantelpiece that
cut time into thin blue strands, blue strings deprived of
oxygen.

Hung from the meat rack a mannequin catches me
staring. Motionless,
we push comfort into puncture wounds dug
by Remorse.

A red hearse
trundles past the roiling waves of wheat outside.
(We watch my blood pool out, my
penance/untether the tenants in the attic...
i'll become mechanical.)
Opposite,
the hearse sends ways
for false assumptions.

THE CROWS OF AFTER

i sink un enfant in the grave.
Dangerous practices. The bones we unearth clutter
grain-killers/slate-coloured machines.
i feel real.

Real is what flows through wind-gusts, a homogeneous
mixture of quick heartbeats and cerebral fluid,
frothed by falls.

i fall, i slip from bitter hands of laughter to
disasters, i'm incompetent, a rupture in
these silhouettes of silence.

Reverence for the corpse
reverence for the statues that line
the walls of this house.

My happy house.

i guideless stumble through
expressions of the face
while crow claws lengthen, rip into my vision
of contentedness. Only certitude is real

Evil—the Crows

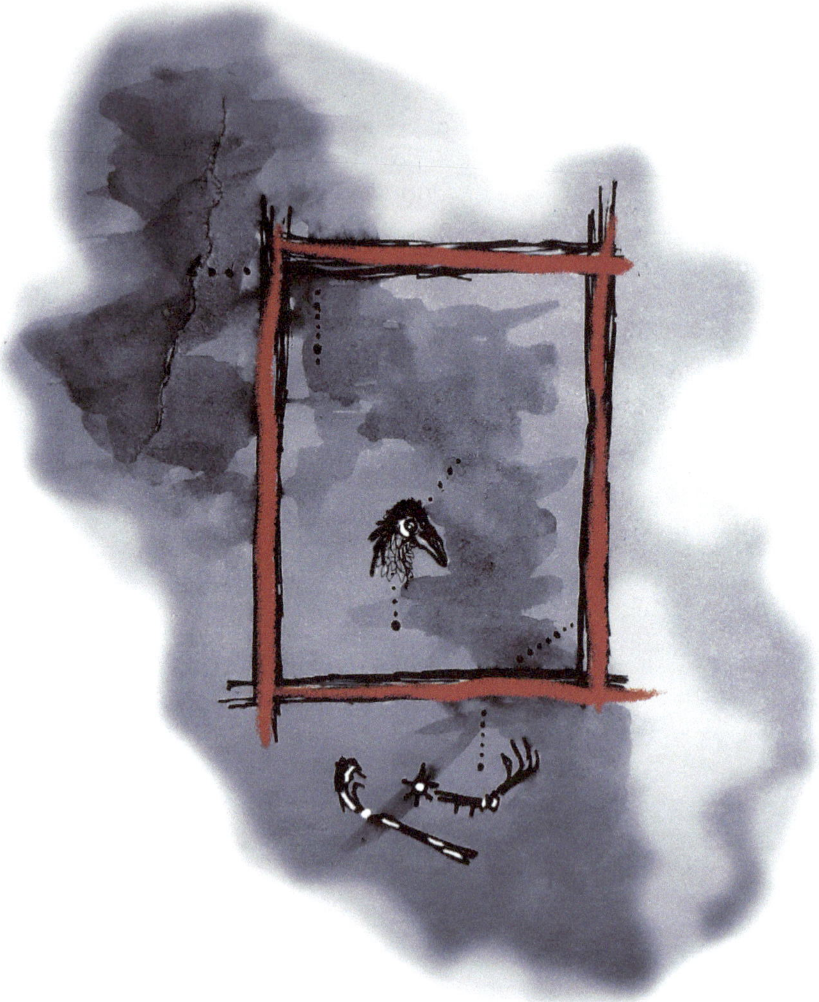

Source

Astral project.
i force every finger,
each feeling
into the sky.

Little escapes
are welcome
progressions.

Taste the fluidity,
the buzzing duality.
This thing has offered
the candy to fly.

Stranger in residence
i cannot stay one way
confusing astral fingers drag me inside-out
(confusing thoughts imploring me to stay)

Whisper of Fancy

It is difficult,
to find in that abyss of nerve dead hope
a single word to bring on anything but folly

grains fall,
all unaccounted for in smoke of colour and noise
lifeless, yet imbued with rains transcending folly

rags doll armadas, mercenaries of procrastination
limply struggle to catch hold of simple thought,
while dreamers drown in folly

all in vain,
the lifeless forms command more terror than the
clowns of nightmares, senseless/sensing folly.

Desire demise in the leaves for the *arbres*
will have no reprieve past the spectre
of doubt and my folly

Bread

Why can't i look away?
Am i bewitched between the slices of your horrors?
Mildew is your middle name in that
it makes my heart beat so unevenly, the thinly
spread molasses
pulling me away—
why am i floating, drying in the sun?
The jerky on your plate
is reddened, burned in shame against the stares of
perpetuity—

my screaming is my
fear
why do you say i don't go out/
i do/i stay in bed
(cherche sous le lit—y a-t-il des monstres?)
Where are you now? Please disappear,
my stomach twisting in the clouds.
It's eager to rise in and make a mess of acid, know
i've died! Don't dare come at me from behind, i'm
scared

Awake

A sound shudders through the room. Blankness disturbs the swaying frequency at breakfast, cardboard in place of cereal.

They rise without moving, the Shadows. Des invités to sit with us today. A special day.

They left the gate ouverte au monde.

Reminders that the world
is paper.
Cease to sleep i
ask to feel Pain again
but lifeless ceased
to be.

i'm split/i'm stuck.
The crows take us as prey/ i cower in the face
     of bitter words (the truths) their eyes convey.

I purge
their love,
now
je déteste
mes regrets.

Remorse
pulls back. She writhes
as her foundations

FALL

collapsed
on paper
dolls.

Ditty

Scrapbook blown apart, ink
plasters our faces...
I crawl between the pages

in the papers.
(They say the world is coming undone.)
//Last evening I sang a ditty
I dropped the trophy too heavy to drink from.
Reached into the void to produce
the fear of another *****

I
consume
strawmen,
changelings, monsters,
spoiled crawlspace corpses.

Clean the dirt off the walls
with hot water/
dissolve
acrid doubt with their bones.

Ditty.
Ma petite chanson
de victoire...

Still trapped.
Still trapped.

Ditty.
My ditty.

Les autres vont recommencer

Tout un Monde dans ma Main Gantée

Les dieux s'affrontent avec mes vieilles poupées,
leurs lèvres peintes la couleur de leurs crimes
ensemble ils sont tous des meurtriers/
ensemble ils ont peur d'être oubliés.
Robés en vert, en verre embouteillés,
ils posent des vers de terre sur leurs frontières
qui mettent des gouffres dans la terre saignée
qui ne remarquent jamais leur saleté.
Ils sont comme des bateaux coulants
les dieux, les vers et mes poupées/
je les noie dans mon subconscient
demain j'espère les oublier

CRAWLSPACE CREATURES

The Art of Contagion

Gophers dart through the field, worn saddles evading
my thoughts, mingling with fairy-sized loads, wind-up
toys crinkling with jagged steps, tripping over their
crinoline dresses.

Diurnal yet dark, they s-shape into my head through
my eyes, a long queue replacing
Remorse to the beating of
aqueous fluid.

Tongue-flicks describe the heat waves
trailing after motion. A silent
film gone herping in my mind, searching
for intrusive snake-like thoughts,
forming a line at the post office.

The necrotic venom of my doubts makes me deserve
what I incentivized. Remorse and I, we grew docility
into a migraine, clouded out the hollow eyes of crows.

I fill my mouth,
lay back.
I'm full.

Rain Viewing

Mist turns to fog
and searching elephants;
the world is softly greying,
treeline, sightline swaying into dark.

Blurry vision is a method to division to
delusion in the equinox of time.
Unlock the organ box;
I swing around a
locket singing harmony and spilling
omnipresent silver leaves that glisten
with the tears of wax and powdered lilac,
bitter rows of false nostalgia kneeling
with the dolls
on snake-shed floor.

How softly do they grieve
when ghosts are dancing...

Digest

The Earth opens its mouth
to swallow my corpse
and digests it, writhing with
maggots.
Soon enough
the Earth
will open its mouth again,
an empty, ravenous mirror of the pitcher plant
I left for starving
on the windowsill.
(A pantomime, perhaps?
The past no longer looks as it should.)
It is tempting to take the plant and
dash the ugly flower pot, to
smash the tiles with it, destroying a dance
for the shock in the face of the sandpapered doll,
in case she decides to be real again,
crawling back from the Earth, up
the stilts of my house
as it opens its mouth
to take one more bite.

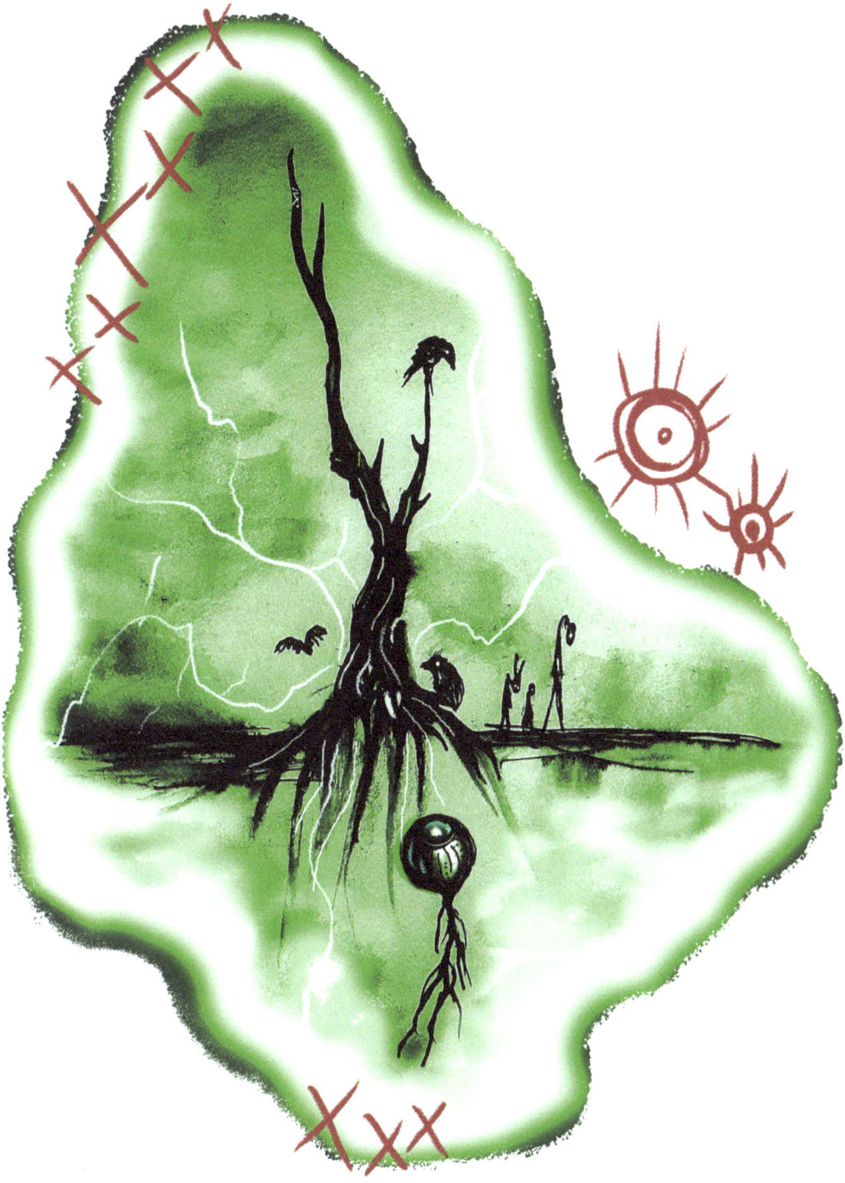

Maggots Rise

They push through the crumbling dirt
that gives way to their senses, seeking out
the illustrious meal of the freshly deceased.
Are they searching to get somewhere/charged
for defiling the corpse, as they
investigate the injuries that drew them to it?
At first they only spelled their names in blood.
What do I own, destroyed by their device?

I recognize in them
the melted figures molded by Remorse.
(Their faces locked in agony while
their outer layers bubble in blisters.)

Was that so long ago?

They've changed as well, mutated, morphed their
grubby shapes to concrete gravediggers, a sworn-in
swarm, the nameless

cannibals.

They hold both sides of the circle.
Their right, their wrong fades out in
undulating disgust.

THE CROWS OF AFTER

Green smiles rise with the larvae as they encounter
their birthright, their stolen property.
Darkened masses mark their crops,
bringing them into the third instar.

They turn to the mud,
burrowing, dancing deeper into the ground.
They leave the nest.

As they float off they trail carrion,
some remnants of human
when all is gone.

Haunt

The night, it is mine,
collapsed in my palm.
A lamb to caress, to cajole
and to twist, to lure and to squander, a nightmare...

A blanket to plague and to bend out of shape,
to freeze and to slip and to settle beneath
a child to terrify out of its sleep
a whisper and scream and a "Who's there?"

collapsed in my palm
is a pile of stars, collected together
and crushed into dust. Forevers and Afters
are lost to the rust.
(To forces and dust they are lost.)

In the streets I drop tears, deep gravity voids.
I banter and swing swords and steal nerves and
rift worlds in answer to candles left lit.
Only now do I know that Wee Willie Winky
holds nothing to this kind of bliss.

THE CROWS OF AFTER

(A swish of my cape,
my claw in the shadows)

my prize is right there,
for their fear,
for the taking.

The night,
it is mine
for the taking.

After

How silent you are
you mighty, empty hall,
where never whisper spoke or
ever footstep trod.

Your silence aged as would the finest wine;
it is complete, concealing shuffled feet between
your expectations. Every distant symphony and
unstitched seam is cursed and out of place within
the thrall of this majestic, yet abandoned hall.

Oh wretched silence,
speak to me a word!
A thought to tell me that in you there be
still fruit, just ripened on the branch,
just low enough to offer me your memory...

But no reply will ever break
the continuity of fruit long withered
into desert dust.

Softly, silently, the snow unheard here falls,
as did the empire from the depths
of this abandoned hall.

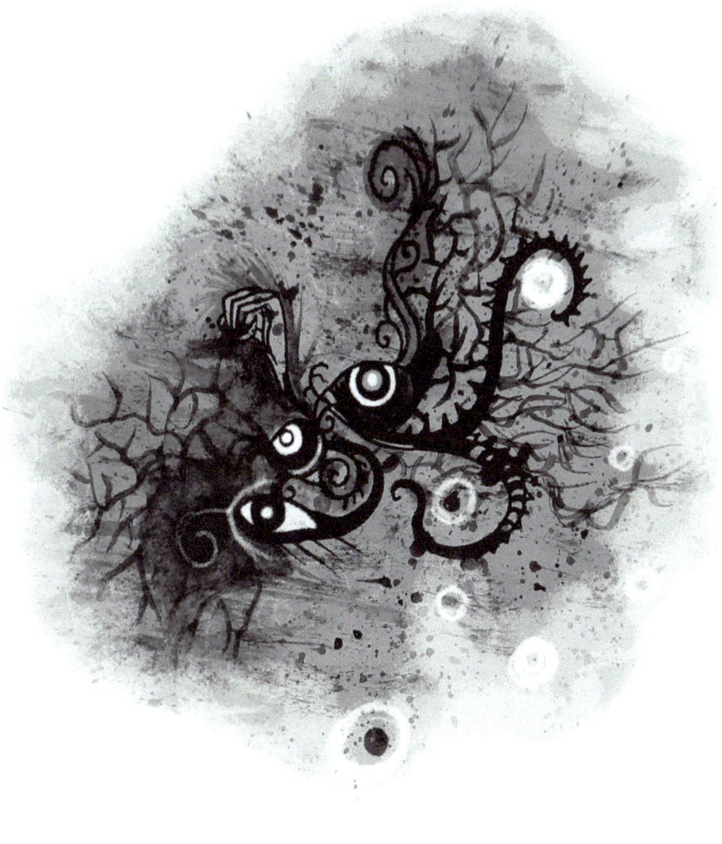

Scavengers

Pity those who live.
I see the future in the eyes of crows.
The four and I are one.

We peel wooden flesh, the muscles underneath
are only sawdust but we feel alive,
alive in our destruction.

We stain the future present. All the past was just
a broken cycle. It became Forgiveness letting loose
her flames again

in fields culled by sun. Her drafted fingers
splinter this eternal house of dreams,
my infernal house of horrors.

The mechanical nurse can't run, can't scream,
can only creak, can never shut her eyes.

We paint them blue together, the crows and I,
paint them shut

but even in death the rusted doll doesn't
seem to ever have been alive so we use
her charred metal arm
to scratch away at the dirt and exhume
Exhilaration.

Not one of any of the dolls remains
to pity, mourn under the rain.
            Not one, not me remains except
                the Crows of After.

Evil—the dolls.
Evil—the house.

I weep for the Crows.

The evil was I

END

The Quatre Crows
Les Four Corbeaux

Thearie, Edmund, Axel, Twit
four times crow and eight times wit
arrogant, doubtful, tired, hit
patient, dire, charming, split

Acknowledgements

I'd like to thank my mother for lending me her skills in typesetting and graphic design, as well as for putting up with me through every iteration of the creative process.

In addition I owe many, many thanks to Luscinia Kay, my editor, for going over every word and punctuation mark and helping me choose the best ones.

Lastly, I'd like to thank the French teachers who corrected my grammar and the English teachers who convinced me to write the darn thing in the first place.

The Author

Exsanguine Hart is a scribbler with an obnoxiously pretentious pseudonym living somewhere in Canada with two cats, an assemblage of dolls and a number of dragons. Hart can be found online either doodling on instagram @exsanguine_hart or lurking on exsanguinehart.com

Specimen SandWitch Press

Specimen SandWitch Press was created by Exsanguine Hart and Luscinia Kay to put odd things (like this book) into the universe in the hopes that they would find their way to someone like you.

Follow SSWP on Instagram @specimensandwitch
or visit our website, specimensandwitch.com

CPSIA information can be obtained
at www.ICGtesting.com
Printed in the USA
BVHW020041080622
639183BV00001B/7